Discipleship

IN THE AGE OF

DISTRACTION

Sheryl L.W. Barnes

To My Dear Ruby
May His peace always
Keep you !.
Rev. Dr. Sheryl Barnes

WW
WISDOM WORD PUBLICATIONS

ISBN# 978-0-9748629-5-8

Published by Wisdom Word Publications

A Division of Sterling-Xavier Consulting Group, LLC

www.sterling-xavier.com

P.O. Box 3605

Woodbridge, Connecticut 06525

DEDICATION

To my amazing and anointed husband,
Linwood E. Barnes.
You are God's gift to me in this blessed season of my life and I
love you dearly.
To my biological family and to my Christian family, I love you
and
I thank you for loving me!

TABLE OF CONTENTS

INTRODUCTION

A Christian disciple, one who follows Christ, can expect to encounter distractions as a part of his or her reality. An understanding of basic distractions can help a Christian disciple anticipate, defuse and dismantle the myriad distractions sure to come his or her way. In the 21st century many Christians are experiencing a greater infusion of relativism, carnality, apathy, compromise and casualness in their covenant relationship. There is a decreased emphasis on God's holiness, commands, statutes and standards for spiritual, civic and moral behavior. Scriptures are being manipulated to highlight what many individuals 'wish' was true instead of what is recorded as Biblically-true. Even well-meaning, mature and committed Christians are being distracted by increasing influences both within and outside of the Church body.

The Bible is the inspired Word of God. Because there is nothing new under the sun, the distractions of the 21st century, when subjected to a process known as *root cause analysis*, are exposed as being the same temptations that Christians faced two thousand years ago. These are the very distractions warned about in Scriptures. The antidotes for distractions, therefore, are found in Scriptures.   My purpose in writing this book is three-fold: (a) to explore the questions of what is Christian discipleship and what distractions challenge such covenant relationships; (b) to explain the reasons for, and effects of, the distractions; and (c) to present Biblical antidotes for the distractions accompanied by Word-based affirmations and devotional prayers.

As you read further it is my hope that you will reflect upon your own personal relationship with Christ and think about whether or not distractions are creeping into your covenant relationship. If so, it is my prayer that you will take to heart the ways in which distractions can be avoided or overcome based upon the Word of God.

PREFACE

"They are so easily distracted."

At the time of this writing I have served for well over twenty years in Christian Church ministry. Because I was ordained in 1998, the overwhelming majority of my Christian service has been as an *ordained* servant – which simply means that those in authority over me (my Pastors and the Elders of the Church) recognized my gifts; approved the demonstration of an ability to rightly use those gifts as a servant; confirmed that God had indeed called me to a particular service; and agreed that I possessed the needed maturity, humility and consistency to be so ordained (publically recognized) as a servant of Jesus Christ in the office of a Teacher according to Ephesians 4:11-12.

Over the years, I have seen Christians waver in their walk, struggle to sustain their faith, and become disoriented, disabled and dizzy from a debilitating 'double-mindedness' spoken of in the New Testament:

> *(5) If any of you lacks wisdom, let him ask of God, who gives to all liberally and without reproach, and it will be given to him. (6) But let him ask in faith, with no doubting, **for he who doubts** is like a wave of the sea driven and tossed by the wind. (7) For let not that man suppose that he will receive anything from the Lord; (8)*

*he is **a double-minded man, unstable in all his ways.***
(James 1:5-8, emphasis added)

Some of the questions that have plagued me have been: "How does a person who begins the journey of new life as a Christian (excited, grateful, sold-out and on fire for the Lord) so quickly thereafter experience setbacks and loss of hard-earned holy ground? Why do so many 'casualties of war' besiege the army of God?" And, "Why are so many believers defeated, in poverty, discouraged, carnal and half-hearted in their commitment to Christ?"

As I sought the Lord for answers I heard Him say: *"They are so easily distracted."* Hmmm... *"easily distracted."* I wanted to know more and that desire, as it turns out, is at the core of my calling as a Teacher (a Discipler) of the Gospel of Jesus Christ and is the reason behind my decision to write this book in satisfaction of my Doctor of Ministry dissertation requirement. What prevents victory in the lives of many Christians has a great deal to do with the distractions we do not anticipate, much less prepare for.

If **you** are curious, as I was, as to *why* and *how* believers, perhaps even including you, are 'so easily distracted,' then you are reading the right book at the right time. The Lord has anointed me to share how the Church (His Body) has fallen victim to all kinds of distractions and how those distractions, left un-checked and un-challenged, have resulted in flocks of distracted sheep. The Lord has also allowed me to understand *why* this is happening, *how* it continues (increasingly ravaging those in the Kingdom), and *who* is behind the distraction. I sincerely believe that if the Church and its people do not repent and renew their covenant relationship of love with the Father, they will be *distracted to death.*

May God bless you as you read this book. By faith I am coming into agreement with all who are blessed to hear the heart of God through this writing and who are willing to repent (turn toward God) and intercede for the Body of Christ everywhere, to attain the wisdom to gain victory in spite of distractions, in Jesus' name. Amen.

dis·tract (di-strakt'), *v.t.* [ME. distracten < L. *dis-stractus*, pp. of *distrahere*, to draw apart; *dis-*, apart + *trahere*, to draw, pull], 1. to draw (the mind, etc.) away in another direction; divert. 2. to draw (the thoughts) in conflicting directions; harass; confuse. **3. to derange the mind of; craze.**

CHAPTER ONE

CHRISTIANITY 101
The Bible is God's Holy Word

If there was such a thing as a course entitled: 'Christianity 101' somewhere within the curriculum would be a discussion about the importance of *believing* the **Bible.** The Bible is God's Holy Word and must be the starting place, sustaining place and maturing place for the Christian disciple. By reviewing some basic truths concerning the Word of God it will make it much easier to understand, in subsequent chapters, *why* Christians are deliberately, strategically and maliciously targeted with distractions. Additionally, a clear understanding of the purpose of the Bible will help you know *how* distractions will show up in your life (and that of the Church), and more importantly what the Bible has to say about each and every distraction a believer will ever face.

First let's look at what Scriptures say about the purpose of the Word:

*All Scripture is given by **inspiration** of God, and **is profitable** for **doctrine**, for **reproof**, for **correction**, for* *instruction in righteousness, that the man of God may be complete, thoroughly equipped for every good work.*

(2 Timothy 3:16-17, emphasis added)

The word *inspiration* comes from the Greek word *theopneustos* which translates as follows: *theo* – means 'God' and *pneustos* – means 'breathed.' Inspiration literally means 'God-breathed.' All Scripture therefore is the very breath of God. When we read, study, meditate upon, memorize and speak the Word of God by faith, we are allowing the breath of God to move through our entire being. As His Word is honored by us in these ways we find that it accomplishes several things, according to 2 Timothy 3:16-17, that are profitable to us. First stated is that Scripture is beneficial for **doctrine**. Doctrine refers to the commandments, principles, statutes, beliefs, teachings and tenets of the Christian faith as established by God. In order to be a believer who has integrity you have to first know what it is that you believe. The Bible lays out the belief system for disciples.

Reproof is mentioned next in 2 Timothy 3:16-17 and means to be **rebuked** or told you are doing something that is wrong. In the Book of Revelation we find rebuke equated with love as Jesus states:

"As many as I love, I rebuke and chasten. Therefore be zealous and repent."

(Revelation 3:19, emphasis added)

Mentioned third is the benefit of **correction** which means to be told the right action to take: the correct thing to do, say, think or believe. No disciple of Jesus has to wonder about whether to love his enemy or not; whether to hold a grudge or forgive; whether to seek revenge or let God handle vindication. All such matters are clearly articulated in Scriptures. When a disciple tells a lie, he or she can search the Word and find the commandment that says *not* to lie. That disciple can be confident that God is *"faithful and just to forgive us."* The Old Testament gives us accounts of real people who learned how to repent quickly and were called "men after God's own heart" such as in the case of King David.

Fourth we are promised that the Scriptures will bless us by providing **instruction in righteousness**. The Lord would never hold us to standards that He had not also provided instruction and empowerment for the successful attainment thereof. Christianity is not a "set-up" to see how much we can guess at, but rather it is a covenant relationship with a loving and compassionate Father who desires to see His children grow in spiritual maturity. For this reason, He supplies not only the instructions but support and guidance from the Holy Spirit to aid in our success. For example Christians are encouraged to *"be anxious for nothing,"* but how are we supposed to do that? The remainder of the verse spells it out clearly: *"but in everything **by prayer and supplication, with thanksgiving, let your requests be made known** to God; and the peace of God, which surpasses all* *understanding, will guard your hearts and minds through Christ Jesus" (Philippians 4:6-7, emphasis added).*

If you have ever wondered about how to navigate the real issues of life: employment, relationships, careers, education, taxes, illness, disappointments and so on, the Bible instructs us to "keep our mind stayed on Jesus" to enjoy perfect peace. It also instructs us to "cast our cares" upon the Lord because He cares for us. We are additionally instructed to "make our requests known with thanksgiving" because our Father knows what we need before we even ask. When we ask, seek and knock it is a demonstration of our faith that pleases the Lord. The bottom line is that ***all*** of the instructions we need are contained in Scriptures.

Here are additional verses that speak to the holiness of the Word of God underscoring how His Word requires honor and respect:

> ***"Do not add*** *to what I command you and* ***do not subtract*** *from it, but* ***keep*** *the commands of the LORD your God that I give you."*
>
> *(Deuteronomy 4:2, emphasis added)*

> ***"Every word of God is pure;*** *He is a shield to those who put their trust in Him.* ***Do not add*** *to His words, Lest He rebuke you, and you be found a liar."*
>
> *(Proverbs 30:5-6, emphasis added)*

*"The **entirety of Your word is truth**, and every one of Your righteous judgments endures forever."*

  (Psalm 119:160, emphasis added)

*"Your word **is truth**."*

  (John 17:17, emphasis added)

*"For the word of God is **living and powerful**."*

  (Hebrews 4:12, emphasis added)

"As newborn babes, desire the pure milk of the word, that you may grow thereby."

  (1 Peter 2:2)

"Your word is a lamp to my feet and a light to my path."

  (Psalm 119:105)

"Your word I have hidden in my heart, that I might not sin against You".

  (Psalm 119:11)

*"And **the Word became flesh** and dwelt among us, and we beheld His glory, the glory as of the only begotten of the Father, full of grace and truth."*

  (John 1:14, emphasis added)

From these selected Scriptures we are wise to keep in mind that God's word is His very breath. He inspired some forty individuals to record His thoughts, ideas, promises, commands, laws and plans over a span of 1600 years. It is not 'okay' for us to skip over the parts we find challenging or difficult in the Bible, nor can we *add* or *subtract* Scriptures for convenience sake. God gave us His word for our benefit and we can rest assured that it is pure and true and powerful! Once we truly believe that the Bible is God's instruction manual for Christian living we will understand why it is extremely difficult to overcome distractions without God's word leading and guiding our spirit every step of the way.

An AFFIRMATION to Declare

"I grow in knowledge, wisdom and understanding
as I spend time in the Word of God.
I understand that the Word of God reveals the will of God."

Let us pray...

"Dear Heavenly Father,
Please forgive me for not making You the priority you deserve to be in my life. Lord, increase my desire for Your Word. Help me rearrange my busy life to include time in the Scriptures and please meet me there to help me understand the depths of Your heart. In Jesus' name I pray."

CHAPTER TWO

WHAT IS A DISCIPLE?

Before it makes any sense to talk about the devastating effects of distractions in the life of a disciple there ought to be clarity as to what a disciple is. A *disciple* is someone who has accepted Jesus Christ as his or her personal Lord and Savior and who agrees to follow Christ. This commitment to accept, confess, follow, love, trust and obey Christ's commands is what makes one a disciple. In the New Testament, Jesus defines His disciples clearly:

*"If you **abide in My word, you are My disciples** indeed."*
(John 8:31, emphasis added)

"A new commandment I give to you, that you love one another; as I have loved you, that you also love one another. ***By this all will know that you are My disciples, if you have love for one another.****"*
(John 13:34-35, emphasis added)

"He who has My commandments and keeps them, it is he who loves Me. *And he who loves Me will be loved by*

My Father, and I will love him and manifest Myself to him."

(John 14: 21, emphasis added)

"If anyone comes to Me and does not hate his father and mother; wife and children, brothers and sisters, yes, and his own life also, he cannot be My disciple."

(Luke 14:26)

*"And **whoever does not bear his cross** and **come after Me** cannot be My **disciple**."*

(Luke 14:27, emphasis added)

*"So likewise, **whoever of you does not forsake all** that he has cannot be My **disciple**."*

(Luke 14:33, emphasis added)

One of the benefits of salvation, along with eternal life, is abundant life here on earth. Jesus said, *"... I have come that they may have life, and that they may have it more abundantly" (John 10:10)*. This abundance includes freedom from slavery to sin. The Apostle Paul explains in Romans 6:5-6: *"For if we have been united together in the likeness of His death, certainly we also shall be in the likeness of His resurrection, knowing this, that our old man was crucified with Him, that the body of sin* *might be done away with, that **we should no longer be slaves of sin**.*"

A disciple is a former sinner. Sinners live by the world's standards, customs and morals whereas disciples live by those of God. In Romans 3:23 we are told *"for all have sinned and fall short of the glory of God."* Every human being after Adam and Eve has been *born a sinner* since sin entered through their rebellion when they chose to believe Satan over God. We are *born* with a sin nature. Regardless of socio-economic background, geographical location, ethnicity, educational status of parents, family name, heritage or culture – everyone "falls short." Without the new life of Jesus Christ, who took our sins in exchange for eternal life, no one would ever be able to live a holy life. No one would be assured eternal salvation with God through His Son Jesus, and no one would experience the presence of the Holy Spirit living on the inside – empowering him or her to walk in victory.

Sin is anything that opposes God. Sin separates mankind from God because His holiness prevents Him from allowing the unholy in His presence. Through God's gracious and merciful love for His children, He made provision for us to be reconciled back to a covenant relationship with Him through the shed blood of His only begotten son, Jesus the Christ (John 3:16). Jesus Christ paid the penalty **we owed** by becoming our substitute and taking our sins upon Himself. We receive His gift of salvation by confessing with our mouth the Lord Jesus and believing in our heart that God raised Him from the dead (Romans 10:9). The moment we accept Jesus Christ is the moment we become His disciple – someone committed to the life-long pursuit of, and transformation into, the likeness of Christ; someone over whom sin no longer has dominion leading to death. On those occasions when we sin, we now have a remedy through Jesus: we can repent (turn back toward God) and know for certainty that our sins are forgiven. Sin distracts. Jesus' redemptive work at the cross of Calvary freed us from slavery to sin. When we sin it is because we choose to, not because we could not help ourselves. This is a wonderful and powerful distinction that *only* Disciples of Christ can claim.

An AFFIRMATION to Declare

"I abide in Your Word because I now belong to You. Others can tell I am a Disciple of Christ by my love."

Let us pray...

"Dear Heavenly Father,
Please help me to honor You by learning more about you. I do not want to substitute religion for a relationship. You are a personal God and I want to get to know You better. Increase my desire to spend time in Your presence and in your Word. Amen."

CHAPTER THREE

WHAT DISTRACTS DISCIPLES?

The World · Our Old Adamic Nature · Satan

I was led to write this book because the Lord told me that His people are distracted both on an individual level and collectively as the corporeal body known as The Church. I will talk about The Church in Chapter Five but this chapter will focus on distractions in the lives of individual disciples. There are three main **sources** of distraction as well as three **types** of distractions that the Bible warns believers about. In *1 John 3:15-17(emphasis added)* it is written:

> *"Do not love **the world** or the things in the world. If anyone loves the world, the love of the Father is not in him. For all that is in the world – the **lust of the flesh**, the **lust of the eyes**, and the **pride of life** – is not of the Father but is of the world. And the world is passing away, and the lust of it; but he who does the will of God abides forever."*

➢ The World is a Distraction ◁

When an individual accepts Jesus Christ as his or her personal Lord and Savior there is an immediate change in who *governs* that person.   There is also, therefore, a change in *citizenship*. A Christian no longer lives 'of the world' but instead becomes a part of a royal kingdom: The Kingdom of God; that is governed by God. The word 'world' comes from the Greek word *cosmos* and refers to systems that operate outside the will of God. The 'world' has its own customs, practices, value, morals, paradigms, philosophies, ethics and beliefs. It is fraught with relativism, tolerance, majority rule, perversity, greed, violence, compromise and other governing principles that neither align with, nor honor the precepts or principles of Jesus Christ. In the Bible we find several Scriptures that highlight the dangers of remaining attached to 'the world':

"I beseech you therefore, brethren, by the mercies of God, that you present your bodies a living sacrifice, holy, acceptable to God, which is your reasonable service. And ***do not be conformed to this world,*** *but* ***be transformed*** *by the renewing of your mind, that you may prove what is that good and acceptable and perfect will of God."*

(Romans 12:1-2, emphasis added)

"Do not love the world or the things in the world. If anyone loves the world, the love of the Father is not in him. *For all that is in the world – the lust of the flesh, the lust of the eyes, and the pride of life - is not of the Father but is of the world. And the world is passing away, and* *the lust of it; but he who does the will of God abides forever."*

(1 John 2:15-17, emphasis added)

*"These things I have spoken to you, that in Me you may have peace. In the world you will have tribulation; but be of good cheer, **I have overcome the world**."*

(John 16:33, emphasis added)

*"We know that we are of God, and **the whole world lies under the sway of the wicked one**."*

(1 John 5:19, emphasis added)

*"You are of God, little children, and have overcome them, because **He who is in you is greater than he who is in the world**."*

(1 John 4:4, emphasis added)

*"I have given them Your word; and **the world** has **hated them** because they are not of the world, just as I am not of the world. I do not pray that You should take them out of the world, but that You should keep them from the evil one. **They are not of the world, just as I am not of the world**. Sanctify them by Your truth. Your word is truth. As You sent Me into the world, I also have sent them into*

the world. And for their sakes I sanctify Myself, that they also may be sanctified by the truth."

(John 17:14-19, emphasis added)

*"**For our citizenship is in heaven**, from which we also eagerly wait for the Savior, the Lord Jesus Christ, who will transform our lowly body that it may be conformed to His glorious body, according to the working by which He is able even to subdue all things to Himself."*

(Philippians 3:20-21, emphasis added)

*"But seek first **the kingdom of God** and His righteousness, and all these things shall be added to you."   (Matthew 6:33, emphasis added)*

The Scriptures cited above all speak to a distinction between 'the world' and the 'kingdom of God,' and when Jesus taught His disciples how to pray He said:

*"In this manner, therefore pray: Our Father in heaven, Hallowed by Your name. **Your kingdom come**. Your will be done on earth as it is in heaven. Give us this day our daily bread. And forgive us our debts, as we forgive our debtors. And do not lead us into temptation, but deliver us from the evil one. **For Yours is the kingdom** and the power and the glory forever. Amen."*

(Matthew 6:9-13, emphasis added)

Jesus makes it very clear that His disciples are not to love or be conformed to the world and the process by which we can grow in our discipleship is by being **transformed** by the renewing of our mind. For a Christian disciple to attempt to hold dual citizenship, living both in the world and in the Kingdom of God, is distracting. The Scriptures warn against being spiritually indecisive, neither hot nor cold and accordingly, it is not possible to live victoriously in two opposing governmental systems. When Christians cannot bring themselves to make a full and total commitment to live for Christ, within the Kingdom, under His sovereign leadership and government they are severely distracted by what the world offers.

➤ **Our Old Adamic Nature is a Distraction** ◄

Becoming a born-again Christian is one of the best, if not *the* best, decision an individual can ever make. We receive freedom from bondage to sin. We receive eternal life with Jesus. We also are promised abundant life here on earth. The Holy Spirit takes up residence in our heart so that He can lead and guide us, comfort and provide counsel. We receive both authority and power to live our lives according to God's plan and purpose. Our souls are saved! However, even with a saved soul, we still have an internal battle that rages that is best explained by the Apostle Paul. He writes:

> *"For what I am doing, I do not understand, For what I will to do, that I do not practice; but what I hate, that I*

do. If, then, I do what I will not to do, I agree with the law that it is good. But now, it is no longer I who do it, but sin that dwells in me. For I know that in me (that is, in my flesh) nothing good dwells; **for to will is present with me, but how to perform what is good I do not find.** *For the good that I will to do, I do not do; but the evil I will not to do, that I practice. Now if I do what I will not to do, it is no longer I who do it, but sin that dwells in me. I find then a law, that evil present with me, the one who wills to do good. For I delight in the law of God according to the inward man.* **But I see another law in my members, warring against the law of my mind, and bringing me into captivity to the law of sin which is in my members.** *O wretched man that I am! Who will deliver me from this body of death? I thank God – through Jesus Christ our Lord! So then, with the mind I myself serve the law of God, but with the flesh the law of sin."* *(Romans 7:15-25, emphasis added)*

What the Apostle Paul is describing here can help us understand that we have within us a desire to do wrong that constantly opposes the Spirit of God who resides within us. This is an important point because not all Christians understand that they will experience this conflict even as they make progress in their spiritual growth and development. When faced with desires that are contrary to God's will for us as His disciples, we are instructed to *"walk in the Spirit, and you shall not fulfill the lust of the flesh. For the flesh lusts against the Spirit, and the Spirit against the flesh; and these are contrary to one another, so that you do not do the things that you wish" (Galatians 5:16-17).*

Imagine for a moment that you are driving across the country and you suddenly see the flashing lights of police cars up ahead. As you slow your vehicle officers approach your window and explain that there is a bridge ahead that has completely collapsed; all traffic is being re-routed around the downed bridge. Would you ignore the officers and speed up in the direction of the collapsed bridge, plunging your vehicle into a raven over which the bridge once spanned? Of course not! You would follow the safety of the alternate route. Scriptures warn about the 'sin nature' within us, also called the Adamic nature because Adam rebelled against God in spite of being commanded not to eat of a particular tree. In *Galatians 5:19–21, 26* we are warned about dangers 'up ahead' when our 'flesh' (sinful desires) gets acted upon:

> *"Now **the works of the flesh** are evident, which **are adultery, fornication, uncleanness, lewdness, idolatry, sorcery, hatred, contentions, jealousies, outbursts of wrath, selfish ambitions, dissensions, heresies, envy, murders, drunkenness, revelries**, and the like; of which I tell you beforehand, just as I also told you in time past, that **those who practice such things will not inherit the kingdom of God. Let us not become conceited,***

provoking one another, envying one another" (emphasis added).

The sinful nature of mankind, including Disciples of Christ, serves as a distraction.

➤ Satan is a Distraction ◄

Satan, who hates mankind and is jealous of the unique attributes we share with the Father, has been on a mission since his fall from grace to destroy the relationship disciples have with Jesus. The Bible tells us that Satan comes to *"kill, steal and destroy" (John 10:10)* and Jesus says of him:

> *"He was **a murderer** from the beginning, and does not stand in the truth, because there is not truth in him. When he speaks a lie, he speaks from his own resources, for **he is a liar and the father of it."***
> *(John 8:44, emphasis added)*

Elsewhere in the Bible Satan is called our adversary, the devil, serpent, tempter, dragon, and accuser:

> *"Be sober, be vigilant; because **your adversary the devil** walks about like a roaring lion, **seeking whom he may devour. Resist him**, steadfast in the faith..."*
> *(1 Peter 5:8-9, emphasis added)*

*"Now the **serpent** was more cunning than any beast of the field which the LORD God had made."*
(Genesis 3:1, emphasis added)

*"So the LORD God said to the **serpent**; 'Because you have done this, **You are cursed** more than all cattle, and more than every beast of the field; on your belly you should go, and you shall eat dust all the days of your life. And I will put enmity between you and the woman, and between your seed and her Seed; He shall bruise your head, and you shall bruise His heel."*
(Genesis 3:14-15, emphasis added)

*"Then Jesus was led up by the Spirit into the wilderness to be tempted by **the devil**. And when He had fasted forty days and forty nights, afterward He was hungry. Now when **the tempter** came to Him, he said, "If you are the Son of God, command that these stones become bread."*
(Matthew 4:1-3, emphasis added)

*"And when war broke out in heaven: Michael and his angels fought with **the dragon**; and **the dragon and his angels** fought, but they did not prevail, nor was a place found for them in heaven any longer. So **the great dragon** was cast out, that **serpent of old, called the Devil and Satan**, who deceives the whole world; he was cast to the*

*earth, and his angels were cast out with him. Then I heard a loud voice saying in heaven, 'Now salvation, and strength, and the kingdom of our God, and the power of His Christ have come, for **the accuser of our brethren**, who accused them before our God day and night, has been cast down.'"*

(Revelation 12:7-10, emphasis added)

*"He who sins is of **the devil**, for **the devil** has sinned from the beginning. For this purpose the Son of God was manifested, that He might destroy the works of **the devil**."*

(1 John 3:8-9, emphasis added)

Disciples of Christ have a real enemy who will do everything in the limited amount of time he has left, before he is judged, condemned and eternally sentenced, to *kill, steal and destroy* covenant relationships. The purpose and plan of the devil is to distract Christians in their FAITH because 'doubting' disciples are unstable and eventually ineffective in their prayer life, witness, and work for the Lord.

One of my favorite quotes from Adrian Rogers, author of *What Every Christian Ought to Know* states:

*"Think of **your flesh** as a pool of gasoline. Think of **the world** as a lighted match. Think of **the devil** as the one who strikes the match and throws it. Then you just see how temptation comes about." (Rogers, A., 2005)*

As you may recall, one of the meanings of '*distract*' is **to be mentally deranged or crazy.** Hopefully you can now see how the three sources of distraction, the world, our flesh, and Satan, can pull a Christian believer *away* from the commands, statutes and instructions of God and render him or her *spiritually deranged and crazy.* It is our responsibility to not only be aware of *what* opposes us but also *why* and *how*.

An AFFIRMATION to Declare

"I agree with the Word of God that says
'*God has not given us a spirit of fear, but of power and of love and of a sound mind.*'
I have the mind of Christ and am not easily distracted."

Let us pray...

"*Dear Heavenly Father,*
Thank you for making clear the many sources of distraction: my old sin nature, the world with its systems, and the devil. All three conspire for my destruction. Please grant me even greater knowledge, wisdom and understanding about Your plans for my life. Help me to use the power and authority gifted to me to avoid and overcome all that opposes You reigning in me. Increase my faith. Amen."

CHAPTER FOUR

WHAT ARE THE EFFECTS OF DISTRACTIONS

IN THE DISCIPLE'S LIFE?

In Chapter Three we took an extensive look at how the old sin nature (the flesh), the world and the devil bombard the disciple's mind, will and emotions with destructive forces. This chapter explores what *happens* when a disciple fails to avoid or properly respond to such attacks.

Distractions, in whatever form they manifest, are designed to weaken your faith because without faith it is **impossible** to please God. When your faith is shallow, immature, under-nourished, shaky or underutilized you will have great difficulty **trusting** God. If you don't *trust* God, His Word, promises, commandments and instructions it is absolutely the case that you will not **obey** Him. It is a contradiction to *believe* that you are a disciple and to simultaneously *disobey* God, yet, that is precisely what many disciples are entangled with and guilty of. We want to have the *blessings* of God without having to be bothered with the *obedience* to God. We desire the *hand* of God but really aren't interested in the *heart* of God. If we could magically change Him into a cosmic ATM, vending machine or genie who grants wishes, some of us would – without hesitation.

But, fortunately for us, our God is holy and knows what is best for us. What is best for us is a loving covenant relationship in which we spend the remainder of our lives, from the point of salvation on, getting to know the One who not only created us but who lavishes grace, mercy, favor, authority and power on us as His beloved sons and daughters.

Here are seven effects of distractions in the lives of Christian disciples:

1. **Distractions create Doubt** – If you can be persuaded to doubt God's authority, wisdom and power, you will soon doubt His love for you and His ability to protect, provide and care for you. It won't be long before you question His purposes and plans as well.

    a. ***Doubt is normal.*** As human beings born with an 'Adamic nature,' making our way in a fallen world, it is normal to have your faith challenged. To be an eyewitness to suffering: children born with disabilities, whole countries ravished by famine or the effects of seemingly ceaseless war, innocent people victimized by violence and cruelty, most Christians will at some point question "Where is God?" We *must* remember that our Father created both angels and humans as moral beings with the capacity to choose between obedience or disobedience to Him. In those instances where angels choose rebellion, the result was being cast out of heaven (Lucifer led the rebellion with one third of the angelic hosts. Ezekiel 28:17; Isaiah 14:12-14). In the instance where man rebelled (Adam) the result was sin was introduced with several devastating consequences: pain in childbirth, marital friction, contrary forces in nature, weariness in work and physical toil, and physical death (Vander Lugt, Herb, 2004). Given these demonic spiritual forces coupled with natural forces of sin in the earth, it is little wonder that on some occasions a Christian will feel heavy. Fortunately for all believers God has made provision even for our seasons of doubt. As we remember and rehearse His promises and meditate upon His plans for us we can exit those normal spaces of doubt and rest in His blessed assurances found throughout the Bible.

b. ***Doubt is dangerous.*** Although is it normal to experience seasons of doubt as one grows in the knowledge and trust of Jesus Christ we are not to 'set up camp' in doubt. To do so would be dangerous because it gnaws at the very essence of a loving relationship. Doubt, left unchecked, weakens the bonds of trust between us and our Father. Doubt is a strategy used by Satan in the Garden of Eden right before He called God's Word a lie. (Genesis 3:4). Again, as we remember that God created us with the gift of being able to 'choose' we have to take responsibility for what we choose day by day, moment by moment. A steady diet of the Word of God can help alleviate doubt as we *choose* to feast on God's truths and come into agreement with Him.

2. **Distractions create Instability** – In the Book of James, chapter 1, verses 6-8 we find a clear description of one who doubts: *"But let him ask in faith, **with no doubting**, for **he who doubts** is like a wave of the sea driven and tossed by the win. For let not that man suppose that he will receive anything from the Lord; he is a **double-minded** man, **unstable in all** his ways." (Emphasis added)*. These verses leave no uncertainty as to the danger of being an unstable disciple. We are told that such double-mindedness causes us to be unstable in *all* of our ways and we will receive *nothing* from the Lord! Instability can cut off our provision from God. We need His presence, peace, wisdom, grace, mercy, protection and favor – all of this and more stands to be taken from us when we waver back and forth about the truth of God.

3. **Distractions lead to Discouragement** – Jesus suffered greatly. He was innocent, perfect and holy, yet He suffered for *our* sakes. When we remove our focus from the Lord to a circumstance, sickness, disappointment, loss, setback, wrong or injustice of some kind, it is easy to fall into a despairing

place of discouragement. In Hebrews 12:3 we find it recorded: *"For **consider Him** who endured such hostility from sinners against Himself, lest you become weary and **discouraged** in your **souls**." (Emphasis added).* This verse reminds us that Jesus endured hostility from which we ought to draw courage. This verse also explains where discouragement affects us – in our souls. The soul is comprised of the mind, will and emotions of an individual and if discouragement effectively sets into these three dimensions of a person it can wreak havoc on your decision-making, attitude and personality. It can, eventually, hurt you physically as well as emotionally and psychologically. God does not want us to remain discouraged and tells us to consider Jesus.

4. **Distractions stunts Growth** – A new-born disciple is likened to a new-born baby. Scriptures speak of the need for new-born believers to be fed the milk of the Word until they have matured and can handle the 'meat' of Scriptures: *"Therefore, laying aside all malice, all deceit, hypocrisy, envy, and all evil peaking, as **newborn babes**, desire the **pure milk of the word, that you may grow** thereby, if indeed you have tasted that the Lord is gracious." (1 Peter 2:1-3, emphasis added).* This suggests a progression in development and spiritual maturation. We are not to remain babies but rather we are to progress to children of God and eventually sons and

daughters of God. The Bible tells us that Jesus grew: *"And Jesus increased in wisdom and stature, and in favor with God and men." (Luke 2:52)*. When disciples avoid or reject growing in knowledge and obedience to God's Word they remain as 'converts' but resist further development into 'disciples.'

5. **Distractions fuel Defeat** – God's intent has always been for His children to walk in victory. Throughout the Old Testament in particular, we see direct consequences of defeat being tied to disobedience. In 1 Samuel the Israelites experience defeat more than once at the hands of their enemy – the Philistines. The defeat is tied to Eli's failure to restrain his sons Hophni and Phinehas (1 Samuel 3 & 4). In the Book of Joshua various victorious battles, including the one at Jericho, correlate with God's leaders and people following His commands to the letter. Following the destruction of Jericho, the same group of Israelites experienced defeat in the battle at Ai. When Joshua cried out to the Lord to ask why they had been defeated, the Lord responded: *"Get up! Why do you lie thus on your face?* **Israel has sinned**, *and they have also* **transgressed My covenant which I commanded them**. *For they have even taken some of the accursed things, and have both stolen and deceived; and they have also put it among their own stuff." (Joshua 7:10-11, emphasis added).* When we allow ourselves to be distracted in our focus on

things, peoples, trends, comparisons and the like, we are unwittingly setting ourselves up for defeat.

6. **Distractions prevent Witnessing & Evangelism** – In the Christian faith there is a command given by Jesus which we call The Great Commission: *"Go therefore and make disciples of all the nations, baptizing them in the name of the Father and of the Son and of the Holy Spirit, **teaching them to observe all things that I have commanded you**; and lo, I am with you always, even to the end of the age. Amen."* *(Matthew 28:19-20, emphasis added).* Distracted disciples are unable to be effective witnesses and evangelists for Christ. Because The Great Commission says to make 'disciples' and not converts, it is not enough for us to convince someone to attend our church or meet our Pastor or even join our faith community. The Scripture says we are to *make disciples … teaching them to observe* all things that Jesus has *commanded us*. It is very difficult, if not impossible, for us to teach someone else something we have not bothered to learn and walk in ourselves. If we ignore His commands we simply cannot teach someone else to obey them.

7. **Distractions may lead to Apostasy** – Apostasy is the horrible state of being in which a person abandons what they once believed. Another term for apostasy is reprobate. In

The King James Version of the Bible the word 'reprobate' is mentioned at least five times (once in the Old Testament and four times in the New Testament). A reprobate mind is one that is depraved, vicious, and unprincipled. In theology, it is a mind rejected by God, excluded from salvation, disapproved, and condemned. In Titus, chapter 1 we find these sobering words: *"To the pure all things are pure, but to those who are **defiled and unbelieving** nothing is pure; but even their **mind and conscience are defiled**. They profess to know God, but in works they deny Him, being **abominable, disobedient**, and **disqualified** for every good work." (verses 15-16, emphasis added).* For the average contemporary Christian, the word 'disqualified' does not carry the weight and gravitas of rejection by God but it is a very, very serious charge. Distractions have the potential to move us gradually away from the holiness and purity of God such that we go so far that we become *too far* gone. God can and does turn us over to our abandonment of Him: *"And likewise also the men, leaving the natural use of the woman, burned in their lust one toward another; men with men working that which is unseemly, and receiving in themselves that recompence of their error which was meet. And even as they did not like to retain God in their knowledge, **God gave them over to a reprobate mind**, to do those things which are not convenient..." (KJV: Romans 1:27-28, emphasis added).* We are forewarned: *"Let everyone who names the name of Christ depart from iniquity." (2 Timothy 2:19).*

Weak faith prevents fulfillment of God's plan for your life. God gets no glory from your aborted dreams and abandoned promises. Distractions are a plot against the purposes and promises of God in your life.

Distractions are designed to interfere with what God has predestined for His covenant family of which you are now a member as a born-again Christian. You will be opposed because the transformation into the likeness of Christ is God's chief aim and desire for you. As you are being transformed you bring God glory! You also bless others around you and serve as living witness of the power of God to change mankind. Your transformation also allows you to experience personal fulfillment as you walk in your divine calling and carry out God-given assignments and God-given dreams. The more you are transformed into the likeness of Christ the greater the threat you are to the kingdom of darkness. You are a threat to the devil and all who oppose Jesus Christ.

In order to prevent you from becoming Christ-like, attacks of distraction are launched against you. Now you know why.

An AFFIRMATION to Declare

"I agree with Your admonishment to 'keep my mind stayed on Thee.' It is You who will keep me in perfect peace."

Let us pray...

*"**Dear Heavenly Father**,*
Though distractions are all around me I glory in Your power and authority to keep me in all and through all. Lord I pray that I will not be slothful concerning my covenant relationship with you and that from this moment forward I will endeavor to learn more about you. Bless me Lord to hunger and thirst after righteousness, in Jesus' name. Amen."

CHAPTER FIVE

HOW HAS THE CHURCH BECOME DISTRACTED?

When I first heard from the Lord as to what the title of this book must be, I understood it to be about *individual* Christians. Right before I actually sat down to begin writing I heard the Lord clearly say to me "The *Church* is distracted too." I was actually startled to hear this but, of course, in due time the Lord explained how this is so. The Church is distracted in at least three ways: syncretism, tradition, and religion. Let's look at them one at a time.

1. **Distracted by Syncretism** – Syncretism is defined as the combination or reconciliation of differing beliefs in religion; also – the merging of culture or cultural beliefs. In the Church, there is an unfortunate tendency to mix cultural belief in with the commands of God. When an allegiance is formed to the cultural belief that is equal to or greater than the Word of God the Church is in trouble. Too often the Church is guilty of practices that place national or cultural holidays on equal footing (or higher footing) than the commands of the Lord, for example: observances of Children's Day that have fallen on

Pentecost Sunday with observance of the former while no mention was made of the latter. Another example is the cultural observance of Halloween by and in the Church. Yet another is the infusion of Easter bunnies, jelly bean hunts and etc. on Church property. For the record, I like jelly beans, I'm just not in favor of mixing the pagan rituals of springtime with the holy season and observance of Resurrection Sunday. There is no place in God's Church for astrology, lucky charms and counsel from psychics among believers and while no church I have ever attended condoned these particular practices sometimes the failure to teach how they compromise our faith in Jesus Christ is the problem. When cultural practices seep into the worship practices of God, the Church can become distracted and new believers will be confused as a result.

2. **Distracted by Tradition** – While most every faith system or denomination in Christendom has its own traditions those traditions must never be lauded as equal or superior to the Word of God. When a Church's bylaws carry greater weight than the Bible it is time for the Church leaders to review both and align the first to the latter. If a Church has established a tradition of serving Holy Communion on the first Sunday of each month, fine. If, however, the leader of the Church (the Pastor or Elders) while in prayer, are led to serve Holy Communion during

a Revival Service or during Lent or Advent this ought not to be denied because some insist upon waiting for the traditional time of a first Sunday. A Church body could well miss an appointed blessing from the Lord by being rigid and tradition-bound. Two searing examples are found in the New Testament concerning the distraction of tradition. In Matthew 15:1-3 we read: *"Then the scribes and Pharisees who were from Jerusalem **came to Jesus, saying,** 'Why do Your disciples transgress the **tradition of the elders**? For they do not wash their hands when they eat bread.' **He answered and said to them, 'Why do you also transgress the commandment of God because of your tradition?'"** (emphasis added).* Jesus questions the tradition of the scribes and Pharisees when it transgresses God's commandments and the Church must be careful not to commit the same error. In Colossians 2:8 an additional warning is given: *"Beware lest anyone cheat you through philosophy and empty deceit, **according to the tradition of men,** according to the basic principles of the world, **and not according to Christ."** (emphasis added).*

3. **Distracted by Religion** – Religion has been defined as *man's attempt to define God.* Christianity, in contrast, is not a religion but rather a relationship. When any attempt is made to reduce the personal relationship between an individual or group of believers to a set of behaviors the

result is lifeless 'duty' (known as 'deontology' in philosophy). If, on the other hand, it becomes only about 'feelings' then responsibility to obey is omitted. Disciples are followers of Christ in a covenant relationship rooted in love, extended by grace and fulfilled by faithful trust and obedience. The Church must never be distracted away from its covenant relationship with the Lord. As the 'Body of Christ' it cannot be vitally alive and effective unless it remains in relationship with the Head who is Christ.

An AFFIRMATION to Declare

"I will pray always for The Church. The Body of Christ is alive and well as it takes it leading from the Head who is forever Jesus the Christ."

Let us pray...

"Dear Heavenly Father,
Please bring Your Body back into perfect alignment with Christ Jesus. We rebuke any spirit of syncretism, tradition or religion that has undermined the sacred covenant relationship. Have mercy upon Your Church, in Jesus' name. Amen."

CHAPTER SIX

HOW DO DISCIPLES OVERCOME DISTRACTIONS?

Hopefully by now you are convinced of the dangers of a distracted life for Disciples of Christ. The good news is that there is no danger, threat or obstacle we will ever face for which God, in His amazing love for us, has not already provided a remedy. Here are several ways that disciples can avoid distractions or overcome them once they show up in your life. Some of the following will seem like a reminder to do what you've already been taught. That's okay. Sometimes we need to be reminded of the basics of our faith.

1. **Study the Word** – Beloved... you cannot practice a Word you don't know. Every disciple is encouraged to *"Be diligent to present yourself approved to God, a worker who does not need to be ashamed, rightly dividing the word of truth." (2 Timothy 2:15)* We are charged to study the Word of God because in so doing we will know the heart of our Father. Scriptures not only tell us what to do but how to do as well. The Bible is our blueprint for life.

2. **Trust God** – We can trust God because He alone is trustworthy. Proverbs 3:5 tells us *"Trust in the LORD with all your heart, and lean not on your own understanding; in all your ways acknowledge Him, and He shall direct your paths."* As we trust Him, He will guide us.

3. **Obey God** – There is no point in learning God's Word and His will without a whole-hearted decision to obey Him. In 1 Samuel 15:22 it is written: *"Behold, to obey is better than sacrifice."*

4. **Confess** - If we confess our sins, according to 1 John 1:9, *"He is faithful and just to forgive our sins and to cleanse us from all unrighteousness."*

5. **Repent** – to repent for a disciple means to turn away from sin and turn toward God the Father. When John the Baptist was preparing the way for the coming of Christ he preached in the wilderness of Judea: *"Repent, for the kingdom of heaven is at hand!"*

An AFFIRMATION to Declare

"I trust God and His holy Word. I study the Word to show myself as a workman who is not ashamed; who rightly divides the Word of truth. I confess my sins and I repent. I am an obedient disciple of Jesus."

Let us pray...

*"**Dear Heavenly Father**,*
Please place in my heart a fresh desire to be like Christ.
Meet me in my times of study and guide me as I learn the
voice of the Holy Spirit. Make me over in Your image, in
Jesus' name. Amen."

CHAPTER SEVEN

HOW DOES THE CHURCH ADDRESS DISTRACTIONS?

The Church is the Body of Christ in the earth. Unless the Body follows the Head, chaos and confusion ensues. The Church must recommit to its mission of worshipping, glorifying, and evangelizing the world for the Kingdom of God. The Church must spread the Gospel of Jesus Christ and to the extent that it has fallen victim to distractions, the Church must do several things:

1. **Repent** – the Church as the corporeal Body of Christ, a gathering of saints whose common bond is their fellowship with Christ, must confess when and where it has become caught up in tradition, syncretism, religious activities and programs that oppose a focus on Jesus Christ. Once such confession is made, the Church must repent, turning back toward the throne of grace from which its power is derived.

2. **Agree with God** – The Church must agree with the Word of God, neither adding nor subtracting from the Bible. In those churches where denominationalism has esteemed

some parts of the Bible over others, now is the time to agree with God in all of His Scriptures. *Acts 5:29* states: *"We ought to obey God rather than men."* If any Church By-Laws oppose the Word of God they ought to be corrected. If any tradition, ritual or practice flaunts itself in the face of the Word of God, it ought to be rebuked.

3. **Maintain Balance**: Fellowship – Evangelism – Discipleship – Ministry – Worship – The Church must find a way to evangelize the lost, disciple the converted, provide fellowship to the members, teach and engage the Body in worship, and demonstrate the love of Christ through ministries. I believe that the Holy Spirit will guide every Church in establishing and maintaining the right balance of these purposes. Evangelism without discipleship produces immature converts who are not able to be effective witnesses for Christ. Worship and fellowship without evangelism leads to an exclusionary, club-like society that is not welcoming of outsiders. Worship without fellowship leaves disciples disconnected from the spirit of family that God ordained for His people. Each facet is needed in right proportion.

An AFFIRMATION to Declare

"The Church is Your idea God and I agree with You for its health and vitality. Your Church is the Body of Christ in the earth, shedding abroad the light of Jesus."

Let us pray...

*"**Dear Heavenly Father**,*
Your Church is in need of healing. Please touch us and allow us to carry out the mission for which we were created and ordained. May the Church be a shining light as we reflect Jesus in all that we do. Restore holiness, order, love and balance, in Jesus' name. Amen."

EPILOGUE

Ephesians 4:1 - 16

(1) I, therefore, the prisoner of the Lord, beseech you to walk worthy of the calling with which you were called, (2) with all lowliness and gentleness, with longsuffering, bearing with one another in love, (3) endeavoring to keep the unity of the Spirit in the bond of peace.

(4) There is one body and one Spirit, just as you were called in one hope of your calling (5) one Lord, one faith, one baptism; (6) one God and Father of all, who is above all, and through all, and in you all. (7) But to each one of us grace was given according to the measure of Christ's gift.

(8) Therefore He says: "When He ascended on high, He led captivity captive, and gave gifts to men." (9) (Now this, "He ascended" – what does it mean but that He also first descended into the lower parts of the earth? (10) He who descended is also the One who ascended far above all the heaven, that He might fill all things.)

(11) **And He Himself gave some to be apostles,** some **prophets**, some **evangelists**, and some **pastors** and

teachers, (12) **for the equipping of the saints for the work of ministry, for the edifying of the body of Christ, (13) till we all come to the unity of the faith and of the knowledge of the Son of God, to a perfect man, to the measure of the stature of the fullness of Christ;**

(14) **that we should no longer be children, tossed to and fro and carried about with every wind of doctrine, by the trickery of men, in the cunning craftiness of deceitful plotting, (15) but, speaking the truth in love, may grow up in all things into Him who is the head – Christ – (16) from whom the whole body, joined and knit together by what every joint supplies, according to the effective working by which every part does its share, causes growth of the body for the edifying of itself in love."**

Everything that God created, He created with purpose. As humankind we have more than one purpose. We have a universal purpose, if you will, to bring God glory. This is the chief aim of man: to glorify the One who created him. All of God's creation brings Him glory: the starry host visible in the clearness of a night sky; the clouds that float unfettered above the earth's atmosphere; the mountains that majestically stand at attention in His presence; streams and lakes and rivers and oceans that teem with life while nurturing adjacent fertile banks of flora and fauna. Eagles bring Him glory as do cranes, roosters, robins and mourning doves. Angels bring Him glory and even though

Lucifer led a rebellion through which a third of God's angels joined him – the truth is – they were created to bring God glory and did so *until* their rebellion did otherwise. Likewise man, who was created in the image and likeness of God, created as God's workmanship to do good works selected by the Father in advance, was shaped, fashioned and formed to bring God glory… and did so *until* sin entered his heart.

But man has another purpose. We are to complete the work that *each one of us* has been uniquely graced to accomplish. In several places throughout Scriptures we are told that God gives different gifts to individuals that they are responsible for nurturing, maturing and giving back to God and to others for the up-building of the Kingdom of God. When we carry out this second, more personal purpose others are blessed and we are fulfilled. Of course, because this process involves obedience to God we cannot help but to once again bring Him glory!

My calling and gifting is that of a teacher and so, it is my sincere prayer that in writing this book something that was shared or explained sparked a desire in you *to know God better*. He is such an awesome Father. May God bless and keep you as you grow in wisdom.

In faith,
Sheryl L. W. Barnes

BIBLIOGRAPHY

Anderson, Ray S. The Shape of Practical Theology: *Empowering Ministry with Theological Praxis.* Downers Grove, Illinois: InterVarsity Press, 2001.

Blue Letter Bible
http://www.blueletterbible.org/lang/lexicon/lexicon.cfm

Rogers, Adrian. What Every Christian Ought to Know: *Essential Truths for Growing Your Faith.* Nashville, Tennessee: B & H Publishing Group, 2005.

Ryrie, Charles C. Basic Theology: *A Popular Systematic Guide to Understanding Biblical Truth.* Chicago: Moody Publishers, 1999.

Vander Lugt, Herb. Why Christians Doubt. Grand Rapids, Michigan, RBC Ministries, 2002, 2004.